Peter Hately Waddell

The Parsifal of Richard Wagner at Bayreuth, 1894

Peter Hately Waddell

The Parsifal of Richard Wagner at Bayreuth, 1894

ISBN/EAN: 9783337386689

Printed in Europe, USA, Canada, Australia, Japan

Cover: Foto ©ninafisch / pixelio.de

More available books at **www.hansebooks.com**

THE

PARSIFAL

OF

RICHARD WAGNER

AT BAYREUTH, 1894

BY

REV. P. HATELY WADDELL, B.D.

AUTHOR OF 'AN OLD KIRK CHRONICLE,' AND
'THE GOSPEL OF THE KINGDOM'

WILLIAM BLACKWOOD AND SONS
EDINBURGH AND LONDON
MDCCCXCIV

' " The Holy Grail! . . . What is it?
The phantom of a cup that comes and goes ?"
" Nay, monk, what phantom ?" answered Percivale.
" The cup, the cup itself, from which our Lord
Drank at the last sad supper with His own." '

—TENNYSON.

By permission of Messrs SCHOTT & Co., the owners of the copyright in both words and music of Richard Wagner's 'Parsifal,' the musical themes have been included.

Love-feast Motive.

THE Christian faith always gains when represented dramatically. For the essence of the Christian faith was once a drama. To see it represented again in that form takes you back to the reality, to the tragedy of the suffering Saviour as it was enacted long ago on the earth. It was a small episode in the world's history; but to live that episode through again is the way to realise its meaning.

The drama frees the mind from pre-conception, occupies the heart to the exclusion of all but what is before it, and leaves only the pure impression of the story on the memory. When you wish to refresh your mind again with the simple story of the Gospel, and to realise once more the origin of our Christian faith, it is best to seek it at Ammergau or at Bayreuth, where the wells are still pure and living waters still flow. Having there seen the Christ-life as it was, you have gained an initiation into Christian truth which not even the Church can take away.

For, at the beginning, the Christian faith was the life of Jesus: and a life can scarcely be represented otherwise than in action, in its living relations with men. If you go back far enough,

back beyond S. Paul, you leave behind
you all the systems of all the schools,
and find only the Christ-life at the root :
a living personality which was a revelation; a spiritual character as it spontaneously came forth in relation to all its
conditions and surroundings. Truths
and ideas, which apart from that character might (and have) become false and
misleading, when seen filled with the
moral significance which it imparted to
them are transformed and renewed; and
the beauty of that holiness, which created
Christian morality, takes the place once
more of the abstract conceptions of
Church teaching.

Few people care to realise how difficult it is to keep in touch with the
pure ideal of the Christian religion, the
simplicity of Jesus; and few who seek a

new faith remember that it lies neglected behind them. Our minds in this are no longer our own. We have been born into thoughts and educated into ideas of which we cannot now get rid; and rather than go through the continual labour of examining and analysing these, we read them into the whole Gospel narrative, and are content to take our religion conventionally as we have received it. When by chance we get a glimpse of the simple truth as it was in the mind of Jesus, we feel for the moment as though He Himself were again leading us through green pastures and by still waters. How much more luminous and real the Christian religion becomes when it is seen as the life of Christ! For in His teaching it was the impression which personal contact with Himself made upon the character that was ever the object He sought. He came that we might have life, and that we might have it more abundantly in Him.

The directness of the impression of Christian truth made in 'Parsifal' is heightened by the choice of the subject of the drama. For the story of the Grail is in itself so simple and so removed from all complexities of theological thought, that we are carried back by it as far toward the atmosphere which Christ breathed as anything now perhaps can take us. For, with much contradiction and some conventionality, the Grail-chivalry yet preserved an ideal as the foundation of its faith; and the preaching of an ideal is the original, though somewhat forgotten, characteristic of Christianity. In following the Grail its knights were but disciples still following the Master; seeking the blessing promised to those who had not seen and yet had believed. The holy cup and spear were but the visible remains of Him whom the world had lost, and they inspired the same reverence, devotion, and courage as He had done. The simplicity and sacredness of the idea was the same—devotion and service. The relics were to the knights the symbols of the Christ-ideal; and their worship of them was an ideal— a life of knightly sanctity and service. In whatever it failed, it was true in this: that its inspiration was still the life of Christ; and, in the ages when chivalry flourished, the Grail-worship did more to keep alive this pure and direct ideal than all the definitions of the schoolmen. The Church in its conception of Christianity has followed the schoolmen: Wagner, with truer instinct, has preferred the knights.

There is a unity in ' Parsifal' which is inherent in the conception with which it starts, and which grows necessarily to its fulfilment. Its truth develops by a natural growth; and, if there be any complexity of thought in it, it is as the structure of a tree or a human body is complex: only until the lines of natural growth in each are discerned, and then the idea of the whole becomes simple and plain. In the orthodox presentation of truth we have a theological, not a Gospel, simplicity; the simplicity of an artificial machine, but not of a plant. Its complexity will not spon-

taneously break up or dissolve; it lacks
a permeating clue; its *leit-motive* have
been lost; or rather, its *leit-motiv* is the
logic of Aristotle, not the life of Christ.

But there is a doctrine of life as well
as of logic. To interpret Christianity
as the life of Christ is not to abandon
doctrine, but only to reconstruct it.
For that life has a unique meaning; a
character of unspeakable value. It is
the expression of a self-conscious atti-
tude toward the problems of religion
and morality, and becomes therefore the
embodiment of religious truths. It is
the result of inner conditions and motives which have been consciously realised and mastered; it is the solution of
world - problems, and no mere chance
success. It represents a definite relation
both to God and man; a central view of

life and the world. Its simplicity and peace are rather a final reconciliation of constant spiritual struggles; its purity is not that of innocence, but of moral victory; its suffering is not of weakness, but of the self-denying strength of love; and its faith is no vision or dream, but a firm and unrelaxing grasp on the thought of the Fatherhood of God. The Christ-life, therefore, however natural and un-premeditated in its appearance, implied always a steadfast ideal, and a continual surrender to it of the conditions and surroundings of life. The conditions of life were the sphere of the will of God for Christ; and the beauty and harmony of His life were but the triumphant re-conciliation of self and God. Each gain in the character of Christ meant a vic-tory gained; and the obedience of its

B

last sacrifice was the token of its final conquest.

The Christ-ideal, therefore, implies a character possessed of a final truth: fully conscious both of its motives and its power. It is no visionary attempt at moral grandeur, no fragmentary series of good deeds, no recurring promptings to new effort; but it represents a complete unity of purpose and consciousness of aim. When thought out and recognised it is found to be no individual, but a universal, ideal. The law of the life of Christ is final for the life of humanity: 'no man can come unto the Father but by Him.' The knowledge, therefore, of the problems of the life of Christ is the realisation of the universal problems of humanity; and the power to recognise the harmony of its growth is already the

power to see the ultimate reconciliation
of all things in God. Thought and being, philosophy and faith, doctrine and
life, are inextricably interwoven in the
Christ-ideal; and a new theology appears when we analyse it. For it will
be a theology not vindicated by external
testimony, or the formal deduction of a
syllogistic proof; but justified by inner
harmony of growth and ultimate *self-
realisation*, which is the only proof we
can ask of the truth of life. The truth
of the seed can only be known under the
idea of fruit: in itself it is not complete,
it abideth alone; but when it dies and
brings forth fruit, it makes good the
reason and the truth of its being. The
end was implied in the beginning, and
the beginning is justified by the end.
All is there; the cycle is complete; the

mind recognises a unity. It is this truth
of completeness and unity in the life of
Christ which must be relied on for its
doctrinal proof. It has in its spirit re-
conciled the world unto God; and in
that spiritual reconciliation is the basis
of Christian doctrine to be sought. But
the law of that doctrine must be accepted
from life, not from logic; and the consistency of our theology must be found
in the symmetry and necessity of its
organic growth, not in its conformity
to external standards. Only can satis-
faction be found in a system of truth
independent of laws drawn from other
spheres of thought, and relying for its
cogency on its own power of self-realisa-
tion; rising from itself and returning
again, repeating ever like life the primi-
tive truth in higher forms and under new

conditions. Then there will be no sepa-
rate and unrelated truths which have to
be mechanically bound into a system;
but all development of truth will be the
necessary growth of one principle, each
doctrine of the Christian faith being as
essential as every other; all being made
complete by that which every joint sup-
plieth. The 'Parsifal' Gospel has this
essential and necessary unity, for it is
the doctrine of the 'Parsifal' life.

Grail Motive.

Grail-knights' March.

T is fitting that a musical drama, representing this modern return to the original unity of religion and life, should be the supreme work of one who in the world of music has returned so completely to the old unity of art and life. To Wagner, art is life idealised. And, if the laws of the new ideal seem some-

times lawless, it is only as the laws of
life seem. Art has so often been a con-
vention, a sphere of science to be studied
and methodised, that the introduction
of laws with the freedom and subtilty of
life breaks up our preconceived notions.
But Wagner-music is in this only one of
the tokens of the modern spirit. Its
revolt against the classicality of past
ages is but the external sign of a new
inner life. No change is altogether
negative; though, as a rule, the negative side appears first. No new teacher
comes only to destroy, but also to fulfil.
What is called the modern spirit is a
movement towards an ideal in harmony
with reality; an ideal which is not only
an abstract conception of the fancy, but
which is a new interpretation of the real.
For these are not different spheres, but

only different points of view; in thought
and being, divine and human, art and
life, are but two forms of one reality.
Instead of leaving behind and deny-
ing the real and actual, the modern
spirit seeks to translate and interpret it,
and in this way to take up and restore
the real life of the world, which under a
false conception of abstract ideals has
been trampled under foot. Whatever
the new ideal is, it must find room for
the real life of man within it, and seize
its inspiration in the present experience
of life and the world.

But it is not a matter of art alone.
The modern spirit in philosophy and
theology has been the same; though in
art the change of view has been more
evident and pronounced. In music the
change is neither so definite nor so

capable of description, as the world of
tone is less defined in its expression
than the world of words or form. But
there is the same spirit striving here
also, in the world of impressions, to realise more the actualities of living experience, and offer now a truer mode for
their presentation. It seeks its inspiration from a heaven which touches earth,
and endeavours to reconcile in its own
way all apparent contradictions, under
a new ideal and in a new language.
The problem of life has been stated in
a new form; we have gained a new
point of view, have seen the truth
from another side. ' Parsifal ' and the
' Messiah' express the difference. Whatever each in itself may be, there is no
doubt that ' Parsifal ' faces the subject
from a higher point of view, and one

vastly more difficult to maintain. The mysticism of Wagner-music reaches forth to that which is before, though it may not have attained or be yet perfect. It lays anew the foundations of the temple of Art; but let every man take heed how he buildeth thereupon.

This denial of the separateness of art is emphasised by Wagner even in the construction of his plays. They are no longer a set of melodies strung together by a few incidents of action; but are vital and active dramas, with music, action, and words woven into the life of the whole. The drama stands or falls as one piece; the weak is as necessary in it as the strong; the music has no place holier than the rest; the dream is one and the interpretation is one. But the music itself also is emphasised as a unity

from the first bar to the last. It is a
gradual growth of musical expression
from a few seeds of exquisite harmony
scattered by a master's hand, a few
elemental and majestic phrases, which
under the form of *leit-motive* recur and
re-echo, till at length they are found
blended in the memory with every
recollection of the play. The final complexity of the drama-music is therefore
a natural and inevitable result, whose
difficult construction of harmonies becomes clear when the primary phrases
or *leit-motive* are grasped. There is
nothing unrelated to the rest; the music
is woven, not built.

To describe further the characteristics
of Wagner-music is for a layman im-
possible. To speak of its expressiveness,
its spiritual harmonies, the depth of its

tones, and the variety of its transitions, is only to say what every one can say who hears. Yet, whatever may be said of others, is said of Wagner with a difference. The same words convey a different meaning; for there is a different spirit brooding over the whole. And it will be found always more easy to describe the peculiarities of Wagner-music in terms taken rather from the spheres of life and morality, than from the more limited one of musical art. It is a new spirit and needs a new language.

The performance of the music at the Wagner Theatre also helps to associate everything in the mind with what is exceptional and ideal. It is a place consecrated to the influence of a marvellous genius, and to the production, from time to time in the greatest perfection,

of the subjects of his mystical ' romantic '
music. It is here alone that the last
and greatest of his creations can be seen
and heard, the one we speak of, ' Parsifal.'
In this the religious and mystical tend-
ency of all his other works is perfected,
so that it may be truly called what he
himself named it, ' The sanctification of
the Stage.' The theatre at Bayreuth
stands on a small hill beyond the town,
and has nothing in common either in
position or appearance with the usual
associations of a city theatre. It is not
a place of amusement, but of pilgrimage.
It stands among the fields, and is reached
by an avenue of approach between trees.
Things at Bayreuth are reckoned by
the natural signs of earth and sky ; time
is not thought of. All that you care
to note is that the fields round the

theatre are being reaped, it is the time
of the barley-harvest; and that at night
as you return homeward the full moon
of July is rising over them. In the play
itself nothing is hurried, nothing is
sacrificed to time; it is not crowded
into an after-dinner entertainment. It
demands the day; from four o'clock,
at least, till ten. The theatre is uncon-
ventional; all seats are of the same rank
and price, and have been bought months
before in every capital in Europe. No
forms of show are allowed to distract
from the impressiveness of the effect; all
accessories are of the simplest kind;
orchestra and conductor are alike unseen;
everything is subordinated to a faithful
presentation of the master's views. The
silence is one that may be felt, as the
divine phrase of the 'Parsifal' overture

begins. No singer has special prominence; all feel too much the unity of the
whole. In any of the plays applause
comes only at the end of the acts; in
'Parsifal' it is never offered. The
summons to the various acts is unique
and impressive: it is sounded on trum-
pets at the two entrances of the theatre;
and the few bars of music played are
some typical phrase from the succeeding
act.

Parsifal Motive.

Faith Motive.

THE play opens in a scene of woodland peace and beauty, with music of peace and beauty, in a morning hymn, during the prayer of a pure - hearted knight of the Grail and his squires. And then, when this note of innocence and faith is past, we come upon the characters round whom the action of the drama revolves: the drama of humanity, of sin and of a saviour. It may be

called, from Wagner's view, the problem of pain. The pain of sin, and
the pain of redemption, and between
them the cause of suffering to both,
the pleasure of life, which brings suffering to him who falls, suffering to him
who saves, and suffers within itself until
freed from its own spirit. The tempter,
the tempted, and the saviour all alike
suffer. Each is involved in the other's
fate. It is a real tragedy — not over-
ruled from without, but growing inevi-
tably from within—in which each must
take a part, and all together work out
the unavoidable relations into which
they have come. Things are actual;
as they must be; as we know them;
as the world makes them.

There is here a strong grasp of the fun-
damental truth, that the relation of sav-

iour and saved must be an essential one,
and not an arbitrary arrangement; they
are not brought together, they come
together, they are drawn together. If
the work of the saviour is to be real,
he must fulfil it not as laid upon him,
but as the final truth of his own nature.
Salvation is not something in the air, a
plan to be arranged, a doctrine to be believed; it springs from the suffering life
of him who finds his heart linked to the
heart of his brother-man, knit up irre-
vocably with the world's pain. The
reality of the doctrine rests on the reality of the personal moral relation. A
doctrine without a moral motive behind
it is dead. In this we have the key-note
of the drama to start with: that the suffering of the saviour is as much a moral
necessity of *his* life, as is the suffering

of the sinner; that the saviour only realises what his life is when he meets the
pain of the world's sin, and only fulfils
that ideal of life then revealed by ac-
cepting this unalterable destiny of his
relation with humanity. His life is no
longer his own since he has heard the
world's cry; in that he has also heard
the cry of his own mission. He will
save men, himself he dare no longer
save.

It is this law of the necessity of suffering, in the saviour as in the sinner,
that haunts us throughout; and there
is, therefore, in the whole drama no
note of rest and peace which is not im-
mediately combined and overshadowed
with tones of suffering and pain. Until
the end comes; and the final song of
victory and freedom is the last impres-

sion which the memory takes away.
Nothing, indeed, can surpass the power
with which the music of sorrow and
pain, of hope and strength, is continu-
ally interwoven, and rises and falls, as
at length we realise that there *can* be no
separation till the end come. Victory
alone can set us free; there is no peace
till peace has been won. Only then
can the music soar away from pain.

This pain of sin, this suffering of
humanity, is at the root of all. Amfortas, king of the Grail-knights and
keeper of the holy cup and spear, has
fallen before the temptation of Kundry's
charms: and, like Samson in the lap of
Delilah, has then been bereft of the spear
by Kundry's accomplice, and in the strife
has been wounded by it; a wound which
it alone can heal again. The wound is

in the same place as that which the
spear had made in our Lord's side.
There is something in this mystical description of the sin-wound so pathetic
as to lift it at once above the coarse
conceptions we are apt to form of it.
Here it is not the fact of the foulness
of sin that is suggested, but its secret
source and nature.   It gives little clue to
explain it; as who can?   Yet it clothes
sin with a mystery which it will need a
rough hand to tear away.   For sin is a
problem of character, and a different
problem in every different character.   It
is not something apart, which you can
catalogue and penalise in a legal way.
It reveals itself only as character; we
know nothing of it otherwise.   It can
neither be understood nor treated from
without; and we fall back into legal con-

ceptions of it, only that we may deal with it in a quick and ready-made way.

Pathetic, touching, and sorrowful to the last degree is this disclosure of Amfortas' sin; of the wound that will not heal. Borne on a litter by his sad knights, pale and feeble, overwhelmed with regret and remorse, he touches the heart with a pity which cannot be refused. We learn now, if not before, that there is *no* ready-made way of dealing with sin. You propose punishment; alas! his punishment is greater than he can bear. You may perhaps slay him; he has already prayed that death may set him free. You have not indeed apprehended what the problem here is: it is neither to punish nor to slay, but to heal the wound. We all can punish and slay; it requires a Saviour to heal.

It is easy to 'break the bruised reed and quench the smoking flax'; but that is no saviour's work. Otherwise the drama here might end for you, and Amfortas be put out of his pain. But even he has had a revelation of hope, the vision of a saviour who healed his wound. It is that hope which keeps him alive; and which Parsifal fulfils. It is the promise of one called 'A guileless fool, but by sympathy wise.'

What perhaps impresses us most in this picture of the infirm king is the fearful sense of the inevitableness of what he suffers, the awful certainty of its action. Sin has baffled and defeated him, and stands triumphant over the victim. The past act of a moment has become an unrelenting fate. There is a destiny now coiled about him which he struggles in vain to unwind; and his struggles, being in vain, are becoming weaker and more weak. Present and future are both gone in the past; the possibilities of a whole life swallowed up in one hour. There is in his despair and the agony of his suffering the sense of something colossal and infinite; of what is immovable, irretrievable. It is like one of Dante's relentless pictures: a life wearing itself away in the clutches of fate.

And the whole brotherhood of the Grail suffer through their king. He alone is permitted to uncover the sacred cup, the sight of which gives miraculous life to the knights. And this the sin-laden Amfortas is terrified to do. Every approach to the holy vessel renews his pain and opens the wound afresh: it is

a continual struggle between duty and
pain. A struggle which his own character cannot support; and he is no
longer strengthened by the sight of the
Grail. For the Grail can only strengthen
and encourage the pure; it has no mes-
sage for the sinner. A beautiful ideal
it remains still; but not for the world,
for the saints alone. This had the Saviour of the world become: the saint of
the Church, no more the Saviour of
men. For with the Grail-knights it has
come to that. In a false reverence for
Christ, they have set Him apart and
enshrined Him in their Temple. He
is no longer the son of man, but only
God; and humanity has ceased to know
Him. They have taken from Him that
nature which was 'like unto His brethren,' and given to Him again 'the nature

of angels'; and now there is nothing in common between them. They have glorified their Christ: but they have lost their saviour. Another must come to restore the Christ-life among them.

Religion even to the Grail-knights has thus become conventional; the brotherhood of valiant knights has sunk to a priesthood. Religion has lost its relation with men. The Grail no longer inspires to holy and chivalrous deeds; it is served only at the altar. The king alone can touch it; and when he falls into sin its light dies out entirely. For, if religion can only touch life at one point, deprived of that touch, its revelation is gone. The separation of life and religion is here stretched till it breaks. Sin, in darkening the life of man, extinguishes the light of the Grail. It is a lamp now without oil; and its guardians must go and buy of them that sell. The Grail has become imprisoned and lifeless; has lost the power *within* of reviving life in itself. It is locked in the shrine of its own sanctity, and requires that some one from *without* shall set it free. What was to save the world, must now itself be saved. Truly, it must be that conventionalities come, but woe to that man by whom they come. All things are at a standstill; the world of the knights is dead. The religion of their ideal has overleaped itself, and fallen on the other side. Some new and living way must be found to restore it; to bring back the ideal to life, to the Christ-life as it was among men. Some saviour must restore the spear, heal the king, and uncover the Grail.

The introduction of Parsifal comes just after the sick king has been carried back again on the litter from his bath, with his sad knights following. The contrast between them and Parsifal is striking: the hopeless despair of the knights, and the innocent carelessness of the boy. Guileless and innocent, harmless and undefiled, he has no knowledge of good or evil, no knowledge of men or life, no experience of suffering or pain. These have to be learned later, when 'sympathy' has made him wise. Now he knows nothing; nothing except the name of his mother. The name, alas! *Herzeleide*, heart-affliction; 'and a sword shall pierce through thine own heart also.' From Kundry, who is by, we hear the infancy-story: how his father died, and he remembered only his mother, who kept him far from the world and all knowledge of its dangers, till he was drawn away by a desire to enter it, and how his mother now seeks him sorrowing—nay, has died in her sorrow with a broken heart.

This Mother-influence is the only one Parsifal has ever known, the only education he has ever received. This is the sum of his consciousness, the whole of his inner life. It is not even a conscious thought; it is, as it were, the breath of life. It is nevertheless there; and when he comes to the consciousness of life it will be awakened to its full power. The first impression he has received will prove the most lasting. It is from his mother he receives the character which is to constitute him saviour; his manhood is

perfected by what it owes to woman-
hood. The unity of the two natures
in him will prove them no longer con-
trary, no longer the weak and the
strong, but together fulfilling the ideal
of humanity. Purity and tenderness
Parsifal has received from his mother;
and these, the weak things of the world,
are to overcome the strong. It is one
of the Christian ideals to consecrate
humble and childlike natures, to see
in the child the type of the Kingdom.
But Christianity consecrates them, not
to enshrine them apart as objects of
beauty and devotion, but, by subjecting
them to the labour and pain of life, to
crown their latent strength in triumph.
The final beauty of character is not
the beauty of a child; but the beauty
of one 'whose visage is so marred more

than any man, who has no form nor comeliness, and no beauty that we should desire him.' It is in such a character that the childlike nature is glorified, and for such a beauty that its innocence must be exchanged. And the trans-formation can take place only in the world's fire; for innocence must be changed to holiness, and tenderness to sacrifice. These in the child are fair, but in the man they become noble; at first they are timid and weak, at last they are invincible and victorious. In-nocence must be tried, and tenderness must suffer; and then when one comes who can defy evil, and sympathise with suffering, he 'having suffered being tempted, is able also to succour them that are tempted.'

The consciousness of Parsifal is

awakened from the outside, from contact with the world. Everything within
is unformed; it is the touch of the
world without which startles it into
life. The childlike nature by itself is
nothing; the childlike nature in contact with the world is everything. It
has no impulse or power of its own;
it cannot grow until it is forced to act.
To become a man you must put away
childish things; though only so, that
the child will still be father of the man.
This first shock of consciousness to
Parsifal we see in the first incident of
the play. He has thoughtlessly shot a
flying swan, the sacred bird of the
Grail; for no reason but that 'he
shoots everything that flies.' But
when he is upbraided by the knights,
and realises the sorrow and pain he

has caused, he breaks his boyish bow and throws away his arrows, to hurt no living thing again. Sympathy with the wounded swan, the presence of pain in the world, is the first lesson he receives, the first throb of life he feels. He has met something unknown before, which has broken in on the unconscious course of existence, barred his path of freedom, and asserted a new right,— the right of something else than self. He has met it in the true spirit: by denial of self, and surrender to a higher claim. It may be only a natural impulse; but it contains the germ of what is spiritual, 'to lose our life that we may gain it.' Parsifal feels at least that there is another life outside his own, as sacred as his, to be recognised and reverenced. It is contact with

D

this other life which awakens his own, and it will only be in so far as he can sympathise with it and live in it that he will prove its saviour.

Having found the sanctity of life, Parsifal in the next scene is brought into the presence of the sanctity of religion. He is conducted to the Temple of the Grail, and is a witness of the solemn celebration of the Grail-worship, in the form of the Love-feast, the Lord's Supper. This is the most impressive scene of the drama, and is instinct with beauty and reverence. The music is exalted and grand. Whatever in any religious service might be supposed to impress and touch a worshipper is probably in this scene perfected; yet it leaves Parsifal unimpressed. He is not a worshipper, but a spectator of it all; and it has no

direct influence on his nature. He stands
indeed entranced and speechless; but it
is only in a sense of awe and wonder.
Religion he as yet knows nothing of;
but this is not the form of it which will
appeal to him, any more than the Temple-
service at Jerusalem appealed to Jesus.
At Jerusalem the Boy felt that the
Temple was no longer His Father's
house; and here amid the grandeur of
the Grail-worship Parsifal finds himself
a stranger. The conventionalities which
satisfy *us* are no religion to Parsifal.
The routine of a Church service is a
stone to those who ask for bread.

But there is one thing in the service
that does reach his heart: the agonising
cry of Amfortas. The conventional form
of the Temple-service raises wonder; but
the cry of human suffering breaks up the

fountains of the deep. The suffering of
the world has followed him to the Temple,
and becomes the only revelation it contains. In the cry of pain alone has he
heard God's voice; to that alone has he
felt any response in himself. Religion
still speaks to him through life; it is in
sympathy with that he is becoming wise.
He is no priest of the temple, but
humanity's priest; whose consecration
is, that he is 'touched with a feeling of
their infirmities.' As the pain of the
wounded swan by the lake, so the pain
of the wounded Amfortas by the altar
quickens in him the new religious spirit
and reveals the divine life. That is a
revelation possible without, as within,
the Church; we cannot tell whence it
cometh and whither it goeth. Its consecration in Parsifal is the consecration

of character. He is not ordained to an office. He is a saviour in that he has suffered with humanity; all else is swallowed up in that, and you forget all else when you have felt that.

As yet Parsifal has realised no mission. His mission is created by the needs of men. He has no preconceived and artificial conception of the work he has to do. It grows spontaneously as his life grows, and changes and alters as the conditions of life vary. He has no special function to perform, or personality to maintain; sympathy is his only guide, the only guide he needs. He will claim no right which he has not won, he will use no power which he has not gained. In the meantime the Church has little to say to the Saviour. As the wonderful spectacle in the Temple ends, with the elevation of the Grail glowing with its miraculous rosy light, he is asked if he understands what he has seen. But the echo of the suffering cry is still in his ears, and he can answer nothing. He is cast out of the Temple then as a fool indeed; though the ' Prophecy-music ' is at the moment being chanted above. He has been among his own, but they have not received him; yet the stone which the builders reject will later be head of the corner.

Prophecy Music.

Amfortas Motive.

HE second act contains the Temptation of Parsifal; it is devoted to that alone. You feel the prominence that is given to it, and the position in the play it is meant to take. It is no mere incident; but the crisis of the whole. It is the essence of the saviour's life and the centre of the saviour's work; 'for this cause came he into the world.' This prominence of the idea of temptation in

Parsifal's life reminds us of the same position it holds in the Gospels: of the temptation in the. Wilderness at the beginning, and in the Garden at the end; and the many suggestions of it in other places in the course of Christ's life. The conventional Christian makes no theology out of it, it has no meaning; he is always hurrying on to the Cross. We are all coming to the Cross; but we prefer to reach it by the path Christ trod. For, while we meditate on all that the life of Christ means, we gather up by degrees some conception of what His death must mean. There is no quick way to the Cross; we must enter by the door through which the Shepherd entered. To hurry to the Cross is to find it empty; a doctrine, without the moral motive of life behind. It too

then becomes only an incident, and
ceases to draw all men unto it. But the
Christ-life is not a series of incidents
from which we may select as we please;
it is a growth as of a tree, in which each
branch is essential to the whole. The
Wilderness and the Garden will to all
ages retain the secret of Calvary.

The 'Parsifal' doctrine culminates in
the temptation. Your theology is growing as the play proceeds; and the clear-
ness and consistency of its growth satis-
fies your mind. You have entered into
the Parsifal-life, and you recognise the
necessity of its movement. It is not a
speculation as to what Parsifal might or
will be; you realise his mission in your-
self; his life contains its own sanction,
and moves onward from within. Not
according to fancy, or caprice, or his

own individual will; but because his life
has ceased to be the expression of anything individual or finite, and is so sur-
rendered to the will of God that all self-
will or wish has been destroyed. His
life therefore is its own sanction, only
because it is no longer his own life, but
reflects the universal mind of God. In
this sense, but in this sense only, can a
life be 'a law unto itself.' The sympathy
from which his life springs proves itself
to be a spiritual source, and is so over-
coming all the contradictions and finite
limitations of Parsifal's nature that he is
passing into that oneness with the divine
mind which makes his life a movement
harmonious and complete, beginning and
ending in God.

But is Sympathy a sufficient foundation for a saviour's work? will that

accomplish all that the world demands? and must we not ask for some further token of his divine mission? Yes; if still you prefer miracles to faith, and power to love. But in that case you are yet in your sins, and cannot judge of spiritual life. When you understand that the highest definition of God is, that He is 'love,' you may then be able to complete that thought in your conception of the saviour, that he is 'sympathy.' His only divine commission is in this: that he shares this divine nature. And as this sympathy at first awoke the divine life in Parsifal, by opening his heart in pity to the suffering of the dying swan, and then touched a deeper chord in compassion for the sin-wound of Amfortas, so here it is the same: no longer now a passive feeling, but transformed into *Love*, the fulness of the divine nature, the active principle and ideal of life, it leads him out into the world to seek the remedy for sin-laden humanity, and to suffer what that search may cost.

He is now, therefore, in quest of the holy spear. Armed as a knight, he goes alone; and the unity of the play, as well as of his life, requires that the suffering of this quest be first the temptation of Kundry's charms, before whom so many of the knights have fallen, and to whose persuasive love the king has lost the spear. In the character of Kundry we find again that mystical treatment of sin, which reminds us of the spiritual problems hidden under that name, which the sympathy of a saviour alone can reach. She is represented as a strange conflicting character; described as under a curse. In former hardened days of sin she had a vision of Christ bearing the Cross, and had mocked at Him with laughter. This hardness of heart has become her curse; her sin has punished itself, as no punishment from without could. The heart alone can know its own bitterness, and feel the iron enter the soul. Kundry has realised this; and the pain of its realisation has given her the first hope of salvation. She feels that the inward pain and discontent are tokens of higher things; the entrance of a new spirit at strife with the old; the darkness which may herald a dawn. The Gospel has come to her, not with peace, but with a sword. For the new life is born as often from the pangs of sin as from

the struggles of virtue; sin may mean
life as often as death. Kundry feels that
to her this pain is the messenger of
peace; and already she has begun seeking it, by a purifying service of good
works,—searching for some cure even
for Amfortas, whose ruin she has been.

But Kundry too, like him, is dominated
by her past; and her curse is not easily
thrown off. It can summon her again
to do its will; and 'the evil that she
would not, that she does.' The laughter-
shriek with which she has been smitten
returns to remind her of the demon's
sway, and she gives herself to do his
commands. She too has had her vision
of a saviour, but with a different word
of prophecy: to her it has been said,
'He who defies thee, shall make thee
free.' But for her it is almost an im-

possible salvation. The bent of her
whole nature is to defeat defiance; and
the only aim in life has been to see
men surrender to her beauty. The
stream cannot flow backward at com-
mand; the course of her life is too deep
and strong. Salvation for Kundry is
too heavy a task; the curse cannot by
herself be shaken off. And though in
the appearance of Parsifal she discerns
her saviour, yet the complicated coil of
the world dooms her to try again the
power of her beauty on him, and she is
urged on by the old contamination to
attempt his fall.

The quest of Parsifal brings him
directly to the realm of Kundry; for
the spear is in the keeping of Klingsor,
the evil genius in whose service she is.
But victory is not easily won. When he

has stormed Klingsor's castle, it is only to find himself in Kundry's garden. He comes to regain the spear, as Amfortas came to lose it, yet temptation is to be his lot too. After the battle there is beauty; the beauty of the garden, the beauty of the maidens. But the temptation here is too patent, too bare, to touch a nature like Parsifal's; it must be more subtle to gain him. For temptation can come from the higher side of life as well as the lower; and often the finer the nature, the fiercer the trial. This Kundry knows, and when the maidens have gone, she calls Parsifal to herself, by uttering one word — his mother's name. She uses the most sacred influence for her evil end, and lays her finger on the only spot where his life can be assailed. She is successful: Parsifal is tempted through his mother's name; and in listening to the tale of her sorrow and death, and the blessing she had sent him when dying, he is beguiled into the arms of Kundry. While there, entranced with remorse and grief, Kundry seals on his lips his mother's blessing, by 'a kiss of love.' But the passion of the kiss reveals it, and Parsifal springs from her arms with his soul awake. It is with a re-echoing, never to be forgotten cry, 'Amfortas!' that he realises what it means. It is *his* pain that comes first to Parsifal's mind: he feels what the spear-wound must be. The cry in the Temple, which for the moment he had forgotten, is again ringing in his heart; and the wound which he has vowed to heal is throbbing in his own side. But

E

his sympathy with Amfortas has made him wise, wise unto salvation. His eyes are opened to know good and evil; he understands what must be gained or lost. Yet not for himself only; he feels the spear-wound of Amfortas, and knows that Amfortas lives or dies in him. For Amfortas he is strong; with him he has suffered, and for him he will triumph. The pain in himself is not of sin, but of resisting sin; the keener pain of him who bears to the end without the relief of yielding. In Parsifal's temptation, we learn that the pain of victory is more sharp than the pain of defeat.

Kundry feels that her hitherto all-powerful spell is broken: the pleasure of life has played upon one at least in vain; the temptation of beauty and love has failed. She makes a last attempt, and still from the side of his higher life. This time she assails his sympathy. She casts herself on that, and pours out the tale of her curse, of her sin and of her sorrow. She opens her heart, and asks for his pity, for his sympathy and love. She has heard of a saviour: it is he, and he will save her; her life is in his hands. All her days she has been seeking love; and her sin has been but. the perverted ideal of love. Her best and noblest feelings have been tainted at the touch of her curse. But he is one in whose love she will find rest; let them live and love, and she will be saved. Yes, he will be her saviour too, and by his sympathy and love; but he will save her by a love that defies her, and kills her curse by scorning her power. His love can be defiant and cruel, that

it may be helpful and kind; he is a saviour who demands that the sinner at
least be baptised with a baptism of
fire. 'To save thee also am I sent,' he
exclaims, as a consciousness of new
power arises, and strengthens him to
defy her for her own sake, as well as
for himself. It is a new impulse, a
new hope: Amfortas and Kundry, the
tempted and the tempter, both in the
balance of his own soul, to be saved or
lost in his rise or fall. He is not bearing only his own pain or striving for his
own victory; he is bearing the sin of
the one and the sorrow of the other;
his suffering is theirs, and his victory,
too, will be theirs. And how is he
straitened till it be accomplished!

With this thought the victory is won.
He is armed, for he is armed from with-

in. And when at last, in a final burst
of passion at her defeat, Kundry summons her master to her aid, and Klingsor hurls the spear to make the fatal
wound, it floats harmless above the vic-
tor's head, obedient before his spirit.
Parsifal seizes the spear, raises it aloft,
makes with it the sign of the Cross,—
and Kundry's garden of temptation falls
about her, a brown and desert wilderness.

Kundry Motive.

Good Friday Music.

YEARS are supposed to pass ere the third act opens. The work of the saviour is not the work of a day or the suffering of an hour: it is the consecration of a life. The wound of humanity is not so easily healed; the price of its pain not so quickly paid. 'For their sakes I sanctify myself': this is the spirit of the redeemer and the task he has to accomplish. To die is much more easy. Amfortas would rather die than endure : the saviour must endure rather than die. It is only after the labour and endurance of years that he can say, 'It is finished.' Nor can there be any salvation, except through sympathy with that labour and some comprehension of that task. The salvation which, we are told, lies 'in a look,' is certainly not to be depended on : it lacks a moral motive behind ; it is a cry of peace, when there is no peace. Salvation lies in 'a fellowship with his suffering.' Salvation cannot be 'attributed' otherwise. There is no way in which it can be credited to you in the books of God. It cannot be even an external gift. Similes and metaphors of that kind can never convey the reality of a *spiritual* truth ; and our whole theology is founded on metaphors, chiefly drawn from the courts of law and made to fit into the spirit of love.

Parsifal appears, then, with his warfare accomplished; a grown man now, weary and worn from the strife of the world. For the task lay in guarding the holy miraculous spear in fight, but not using it. He must win in his own name and by his own power. Through these years, while he had the miracle in his hand, often must the voice have said, 'If thou be the son of God': but that too had to be resisted, that he might be in all things like unto his brethren; and, having suffered being tempted, might be able to succour them that are tempted. You cannot have a saviour in other conditions than your own; he must be in all things tempted like as you are, yet without sin.

On Good Friday morning he again
finds himself near the precincts of the
Grail, at a hut where one of the Grail-
brothers has come to dwell, to keep his
knightly vow. For the knights, alas!
in these years have fallen away, have
forsaken their holy life, and turned again
to the world and the pleasures they had
forsworn. Amfortas had ceased to uncover the Grail, and the knights were
deprived of its miraculous power. The
brotherhood was falling to pieces. The
miraculous had been tried and found
wanting; the sanctity and seclusion of
a Temple could produce no religion.
Parsifal must come again, that they
may have life and that they may have
it more abundantly. The divided kingdom must be united, and the life of sympathy and of suffering must bring back

the consecration to the Church which she had lost. The conventional doctrinal religion must be abandoned, and a religion which is one with life must take its place. The sympathy of the suffering saviour must be the consecration of its priesthood, and the real life of humanity must be the subject of its teaching. The Church must be breathed upon again; this time not from heaven only, but from earth also. The mysteries of the divine life are no longer to be secluded in the Temple shrine, and to be uncovered by one hand; but they are to be the possession of him who has fought to win them, and whose guileless ignorance has been changed to wisdom, not by the traditions of a priestly caste, but by his suffering sympathy with humanity. So only can a conventional Grail-

worship be reanimated, and its ideal of
the Gospel become again something real
for the world.

It is to this that Parsifal is called;
the stone is now to become head of
the corner. His warfare is ended, his
victory gained. In sympathy and suffering he has triumphed for men; and
returns now to reign. The cycle of
his life is complete; for because he
was weak he became strong, and by
suffering found peace. In losing his
life he found it; and in dying he taught
men to live. In the service of God
he found freedom; and by sympathy
with suffering he relieved it. At his
touch the sin-wound has been healed,
and the cry of humanity calmed. The
inspiration of a new life has been found
in a living faith, and the hope of the

future in the forgiveness of the past.
Parsifal returns therefore as the king
of the new kingdom; not with outward
power or authority, but by the inward
consecration of his spirit. He is to
reign, whose right it is to reign; in
whom the prophecy of the saviour is
fulfilled, and who can preach 'the accept-
able year of the Lord.'

He lays aside his armour, therefore,
on this Good Friday morning. Everything once more is peaceful and fair.
The meadows are blooming under
'Good Friday's magic'; and Parsifal
finds the blessing of those who rest
from their labours. He is attended
and refreshed by the knight; but
attended also by another. For, as he
wakes from a fainting sleep, he finds
Kundry bathing his feet with her tears,

and wiping them with the hair of her
head. Her curse was removed when
Parsifal defied her beauty; she, too,
in losing her life had found it. And
now one, who before could only laugh,
finds at the feet of her saviour the
exquisite joy of tears. The saviour
recognises the new life, and with his
own hand silently baptises her into it.
He seals her baptism with a kiss, to
purge away the memory of her own.

The three then set forth for the
temple of the Grail; and the unity of
the drama is maintained by a repetition
now of the first solemn service we
witnessed there. Amfortas is borne in
as before, more weary and more despairing, and driven to distraction by the
cry of the knights that he must uncover
the Grail. His father has died from

lack of the sight of it, and they them-
selves feel life wearing away. But
Amfortas is no longer equal to the
pain ; *that* sacrifice cannot be made.
Grail-worship had lost its inspiration.
The news of his father's death is the
last blow to the erring king; and in
an agony of remorse he casts himself
among his knights, and begs that they
will slay him. But Parsifal enters with
the holy spear; and, approaching Amfortas, lays it on the wound, and it is
healed. Then, amid the silent adoration
of the knights and the trembling strains
of a divine music, he advances to the
altar, uncovers the Grail, and holds it
in blessing over them. The dove hovers
over his head, as in his hand the cup
glows again with its miraculous rosy
light, the token of a new life restored

to the brotherhood. Kundry is there
too to share it; but, having seen the
glory of it, she falls dead at Parsifal's
feet.

Grail Motive.

'*And o'er his head the Holy Vessel hung
Redder than any rose, a joy to me,
For now I knew the veil had been withdrawn.*'

—TENNYSON.

PRINTED BY WILLIAM BLACKWOOD AND SONS.

PRINTED BY WILLIAM BLACKWOOD AND SONS.

and wiping them with the hair of her head. Her curse was removed when Parsifal defied her beauty; she, too, in losing her life had found it. And now one, who before could only laugh, finds at the feet of her saviour the exquisite joy of tears. The saviour recognises the new life, and with his own hand silently baptises her into it. He seals her baptism with a kiss, to purge away the memory of her own.

The three then set forth for the temple of the Grail; and the unity of the drama is maintained by a repetition now of the first solemn service we witnessed there. Amfortas is borne in as before, more weary and more despairing, and driven to distraction by the cry of the knights that he must uncover the Grail. His father has died from

lack of the sight of it, and they them-
selves feel life wearing away. But
Amfortas is no longer equal to the
pain ; *that* sacrifice cannot be made.
Grail - worship had lost its inspiration.
The news of his father's death is the
last blow to the erring king; and in
an agony of remorse he casts himself
among his knights, and begs that they
will slay him. But Parsifal enters with
the holy spear; and, approaching Amfortas, lays it on the wound, and it is
healed. Then, amid the silent adoration
of the knights and the trembling strains
of a divine music, he advances to the
altar, uncovers the Grail, and holds it
in blessing over them. The dove hovers
over his head, as in his hand the cup
glows again with its miraculous rosy
light, the token of a new life restored

www.ingramcontent.com/pod-product-compliance
Lightning Source LLC
Chambersburg PA
CBHW022145090426
42742CB00010B/1398